lemon
and ,

y
ms
)

LESSONS FROM THE KEYS OF LIFE: *Joy Peace ,*

RESILIENCE & EMPOWERMENT TO MOVE FORWARD

Coach J Dianne
Tribble

By: Coach J Dianne Tribble

COPYRIGHT

LESSONS FROM THE KEYS OF LIFE: RESILIENCE & EMPOWERMENT TO MOVE FORWARD

© Copyright 2019 by Coach J Dianne Tribble

ISBN- 9781690180814

Printed in the United States of America

At the Table
Life Coaching & Motivational Speaking Services

DEDICATION

Lessons from the Keys of Life: Resilience & Empowerment to Move Forward is dedicated to my best friend and beloved husband, Larry Tribble. Thank you for being the visionary in my life. From our dating days back in 1981 to today, you have always recognized the potential within me. When I was unable to see and accept what you saw in me, it never deterred your steadfast faith in me. Thank you for never giving up on me and never letting me quit, as I figured things out along the way. You've been my Coach - cheering me on, affirming me, and challenging me. I thank God for you. You've been a wonderful husband and father to our children. You have played a very significant role in me walking in my God-given purpose. It's you and me, and Jesus makes three. Enjoy the Lessons I've learned from the Keys of Life.

Joy & Peace,

J Dianne Tribble

ALSO WRITTEN BY COACH J DIANNE TRIBBLE

- ❖ The Star Inside of You: Motivational Nuggets & Inspirational Stories of Encouragement
- ❖ So You Want to Be a Life Coach Anthology (co-written with Gigi Blackshear, Ronline Cannady, Cindy Coates, Gina Jackson, Alvin W.King, Shara Mondy, and Iris T. Moore)
- ❖ Chew & Chat MORSELS At the Table
- ❖ Take Note At the Table

Table of Contents

At the Table
Life Coaching & Instructional Speaking Services
Inviting You to A Divine!

Endorsement

Thought-provoking, memorable, and creative genius are the three phrases I would use to describe J Dianne Tribble's latest book "Lessons From The Keys Of Life." Every time I look at my keyboard now, I will have a lasting memory on how the keys on the keyboard are lessons for me to apply to my life and desired legacy. I recommend this book for anyone that is looking for lasting nuggets to apply to life's journey. ~ **Lequita Brooks, MSW, LCSW Lead Therapist & CEO. Website: TherapyTopia.com**

Therapy Topia

INTRODUCTION

For I know the plans I have for you," declares the LORD,
"plans to prosper you and not to harm you, plans to give you
hope and a future. ~ Jeremiah 29:11 NIV

~

Your eyes saw my unformed body; all the days ordained for
me were written in your book before one of them came to be.
~ Psalm 139:16 NIV

There is a reason why we are all here. There is a purpose assigned to each of us. Finding, exploring, and living the purpose will bring fulfillment in life.

With a world population exceeding seven billion people, according to worldometers.info/world-population/, it is astounding that each of us is uniquely designed and fingerprinted. Twins are not exempt. Identical in features, scientific studies have proven they each possess individual DNA and fingerprints.

While our days are pre-determined, according the scripture, we are responsible for discovering and fulfilling our purposes in life. Our purposes are there all along, but it seems they are hidden from us for us. It becomes our responsibility to find them. In the process, there are lessons to be learned. Some lessons will prove to be easier than others. Some lessons may tempt you to give up; however, it's important to keep moving forward.

Should the over-whelming desire to give up get the best of you and you succumb, know this, the purpose still stands. It does not change. True, the purpose is delayed, but it is not cancelled. Be willing to get up, get motivated, and moving forward once again. I'm cheering you on. I believe in you.

A few years ago, I found myself wide awake around 3:00am. As I laid there in bed wide awake, I found myself reflecting on a couple of business initiatives and the challenges in which they presented. I really wanted to see both initiatives actively working. I went from a reflective mode to strategizing. What did I need to do differently? What was the missing element? What if I did this? What if I tried that?

I finally had to get up! My brain was in overdrive. I walked down the hallway to my living room and began to silently walk back and forth. Initially, there were no words, which allowed my mind to get silent. I began to pray, sharing my questions and concerns with the Lord. Finding myself at a place of peace, I walked into my office and sat down at the computer.

As I looked at my computer keypad, it was as if the keys were talking to me. I was receiving words of wisdom and encouragement as I viewed the keys. I grabbed pen and paper to capture everything I was receiving from the keys. This was the encouragement, as well as the next set of instructions I needed in order to move forward with the business initiatives I mentioned earlier.

My creative energy kicked in. I took all that I received from the keys and put together a PowerPoint visual. This was followed by creating a workshop designed to motivate and encourage others who may find themselves in a "holding pattern."

I scheduled the workshop and shared it with a group of about 15 people at different places in their careers and businesses. The workshop was a great success. Several participants shared how they planned to move forward as a result of the presentation. The feedback was very rewarding. At that point, I felt I had done what I was supposed to do with it in order to help others, as the revelation had helped me. I stored the information until...

Earlier this year, I partnered with a marketplace ministry business owner for an event. As the heart of the event was shared, I knew I wanted to impart lessons I have learned over the course of the past eight years. I pondered different areas of focus but did not have the peace to proceed in those areas.

As I sat quietly one morning, the lessons I learned from the keyboard came back to mind. I pulled my stored materials up. It was like a breath of fresh air all back over again. Just as the thoughts behind the keys had motivated and encouraged me years ago, the same thing was happening again. I knew immediately this would be the perfect material to share during the event.

Most of the attendees were relatively new business owners. There were seasoned business owners in attendance as well. The presentation, once again proved to be enlightening, motivating, encouraging, and challenging. The presentation produced a robust discussion time. I was left with that wonderful feeling of accomplishment.

As I shared the experience the following week with a fellow business owner, I was encouraged to make the lessons from the keys available to the public. Henceforth, I proceeded in writing this book. I believe that all who take the time to read the messages from the keys will not only be encouraged and motivated, but will receive personal messages regarding their own life challenges.

We will all be faced with challenges. How we respond to the challenges of life will determine our progress. Remember, the purpose never changes regardless to the temptation to give up. Hold on. There is a promise in scripture which states, "He comforts us in all our troubles so that we can comfort others. When they are troubled, we will be able to give them the same comfort God has given us." ~ 2 Corinthians 1:4 NLT

Here's to your continuous success. I believe in you. Let's run the race before us, staying in our own lane, so that we can take possession of our prize.

Joy & Peace,

~ Coach J Dianne Tribble

Always be ready to invest in you.

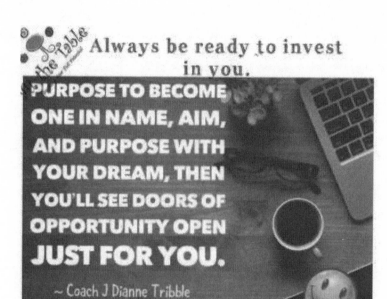

Always be ready to invest in you.

PURPOSE TO BECOME ONE IN NAME, AIM, AND PURPOSE WITH YOUR DREAM, THEN YOU'LL SEE DOORS OF OPPORTUNITY OPEN **JUST FOR YOU.**

~ Coach J Dianne Tribble

www.atthetableinc.com

LESSONS FROM THE KEYS Of LIFE:

RESILIENCE & EMPOWERMENT TO MOVE FORWARD

This is where it all started as I sat looking at the keys on my keyboard.

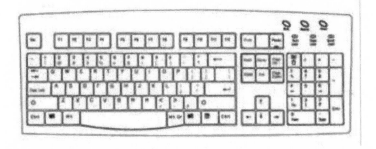

As I share the Keys with you, feel free to capture your thoughts, inspirations, and revelations on the opposite side of each page. Capture what immediately comes to mind. List one practical step you can take based on the key.

KEY NOTES

_____

_____

_____

_____

_____

_____

_____

_____

_____

_____

_____

_____

_____

LESSONS FROM THE KEYS Of LIFE:
RESILIENCE & EMPOWERMENT TO MOVE FORWARD

The Keyboard

Lessons from the Keys begins with the **Keyboard**. The Keyboard represents the community gathering place. This is the location which affords you the opportunity to hang out with like-minded people. This serves as a "home base." You will find your support here. You will find understanding here. You will come to realize you are not alone. Others are gathered in the same spot. What do you need? What do you have to offer others? The gathering spot should serve as a reminder that you are not alone. Help is available from numerous sources and from people from various backgrounds. Be willing to speak up. Let your need or desire be known.

KEY NOTES

_____

_____

_____

_____

_____

_____

_____

_____

_____

_____

_____

_____

LESSONS FROM THE KEYS Of LIFE:
RESILIENCE & EMPOWERMENT TO MOVE FORWARD

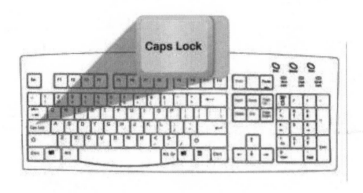

Cap Lock Key

The **Cap Lock Key** serves as a reminder to be firm, to be fair, and to not allow yourself to be taken lightly. This Key is about being assertive. Take ownership of your decisions and stand by them. Make choices which work for you without feelings of regret and frustration. Exercise confidence in your decision-making. Be willing to say "No" when it is in your best interest, without apologies. Set an example. Be an example. Use your Cap Lock Key.

KEY NOTES

_____

_____

_____

_____

_____

_____

_____

_____

_____

_____

_____

_____

_____

LESSONS FROM THE KEYS Of LIFE:

RESILIENCE & EMPOWERMENT TO MOVE FORWARD

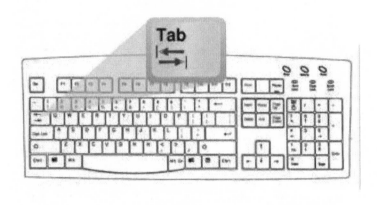

Tab Key

Your **Tab Key** is your humility key. Scoot over. Step aside. Allow others to share the limelight. Allow others to explore their abilities without doing the work for them. Be willing to serve as you lead by example. Give up your seat, allowing others to sit. Show interest in others. Listen well before speaking. Give honor where honor is due. Invest time in your inner circle as a participant from time-to-time, instead of as the leader.

KEY NOTES

_____

_____

_____

_____

_____

_____

_____

_____

_____

_____

_____

_____

_____

LESSONS FROM THE KEYS Of LIFE:

RESILIENCE & EMPOWERMENT TO MOVE FORWARD

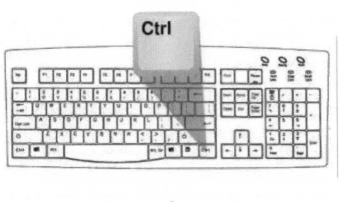

Control Key:

Your **Control Key** sounds the alarm for the leader within you to arise! You are in charge. Make decisions and follow through on them. Take charge of your destiny. At the end of the day, you must give account for your decisions or failure to make decisions. Own it as a leader. Others are not only watching; they are following your lead. Lead well. You have what it takes to take **Control.** Take the reins. You can do it!

KEY NOTES

LESSONS FROM THE KEYS Of LIFE:

RESILIENCE & EMPOWERMENT TO MOVE FORWARD

Alt Key

In order to get results, it will sometimes require you to do some things differently. Maybe it worked in the past but no longer works in your favor. This is a prime time to consider your alternatives. What could you do differently? Be open to taking a different approach. Just as the **Alt** key on your computer requires you to press another key in order to produce results, sometimes we must select an alternative and take a new course of action in order to produce results.

KEY NOTES

_____

_____

_____

_____

_____

_____

_____

_____

_____

_____

_____

_____

_____

LESSONS FROM THE KEYS Of LIFE:

RESILIENCE & EMPOWERMENT TO MOVE FORWARD

Delete Key

Be willing to let them go! Be willing to abandon the old. It is no longer working for you. We have all heard the familiar saying, "Some people come into your life for a reason, a season, or a lifetime." Allow the seasonal people, as well as the "for a reason people" go. You are holding up your own progress, as well as holding up the progress of others. Learn to recognize the seasons and it will remove the sting of a broken relationship. Release them. Let them go. Release it. Let it go. You will be so much better off. It is a process, but you can do it.

KEY NOTES

_____

_____

_____

_____

_____

_____

_____

_____

_____

_____

_____

_____

_____

LESSONS FROM THE KEYS Of LIFE:

RESILIENCE & EMPOWERMENT TO MOVE FORWARD

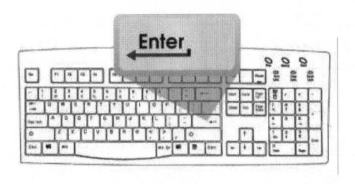

Enter Key

With an open posture, welcome new opportunities. This key is relevant in our personal lives, our careers, and our small businesses. The open posture (with a smile) helps us to be approachable. However, be mindful of those who are drawn to you. This will enable you to discern whether they are good for you or sent to derail you. There are seasons assigned to people. There is a time for people to enter your life and there is a time to release them. Timing is key.

KEY NOTES

_____

_____

_____

_____

_____

_____

_____

_____

_____

_____

_____

_____

_____

LESSONS FROM THE KEYS Of LIFE:

RESILIENCE & EMPOWERMENT TO MOVE FORWARD

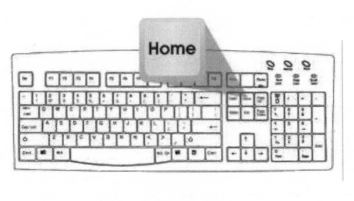

Home Key

The **Home key** is probably the most important key. Home – that wonderful place to exhale. Home is our place of refuge, reflection, rest, reconnection, and restoration. At the close of a busy, productive day, there's normally no better place to be than home. Treasure your home. Appreciate it. Enjoy it. It's your place of refuge.

KEY NOTES

LESSONS FROM THE KEYS Of LIFE:

RESILIENCE & EMPOWERMENT TO MOVE FORWARD

Backspace Key

Life calls for times to revisit areas of challenge. Despite our best efforts, there are times when our expected results do not materialize. Don't lose hope! Many times, we can learn from our short comings. Review the steps taken in preparation. What could you do differently to drive expected results? Be willing to go back and try again. It is an act of humility. Your humility could position you for success this time, as it provides you with experience to share with others who are facing challenges. Go back. Try it again.

KEY NOTES

_____

_____

_____

_____

_____

_____

_____

_____

_____

_____

_____

_____

_____

LESSONS FROM THE KEYS Of LIFE:

RESILIENCE & EMPOWERMENT TO MOVE FORWARD

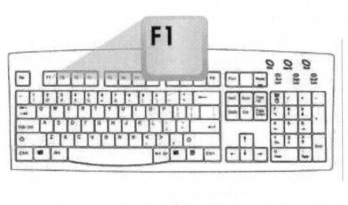

F1 Key

While it is good to research and troubleshoot challenges, there comes a time when seeking assistance is the most practical thing to do. Be willing to ask for help. Resolution could happen suddenly. There is so much more which could be accomplished by partnering with others. The "island" and "silo" mentality could impede your results. Open your mouth or raise your hand. Be willing to let your challenge be known. Help is available. Sometimes it comes in unexpected ways.

KEY NOTES

_____

_____

_____

_____

_____

_____

_____

_____

_____

_____

_____

_____

_____

LESSONS FROM THE KEYS Of LIFE:

RESILIENCE & EMPOWERMENT TO MOVE FORWARD

Esc (Escape) Key

The **Esc key** is your self-care reminder. Life calls for the "do me" escapes. Managing work and life is an ongoing process. We can experience harmony between the two when we factor self-care into our schedules. Identify those things which bring you peace and harmony. Identify those things which leave you refreshed; refocused; and rejuvenated. Make time for these activities. They promote mental wellness and wellbeing. Get away. Vacate. Know when to shut it down. Know when to say "no." Escape and refresh. This will bring clarity of heart and clarity of mind. Sit down somewhere. Release and smile.

KEY NOTES

LESSONS FROM THE KEYS Of LIFE:

RESILIENCE & EMPOWERMENT TO MOVE FORWARD

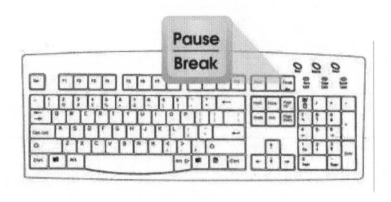

Pause/Break Key

Slow down. Be still. Exercise "The Pause." The Pause is all about allowing yourself to ponder and think before responding. Every action does not warrant an immediate response. Listen attentively and allow yourself to think. Life pushes us to go, go, go and do, do, do! Wisdom cautions us to slow down and consider, prior to making our next move. There is clearly a time and season for both. Be determined to know the difference and respond accordingly.

KEY NOTES

LESSONS FROM THE KEYS Of LIFE:

RESILIENCE & EMPOWERMENT TO MOVE FORWARD

Asterisk (Star) Key:

You are a Star! The asterisk key is a reminder to award yourself for progress. We live our dreams, hopes, desires, and aspirations as a result of the journey. The journey will be filled with many experiences – some good and some bad. The journey will consist of a combination of both. Along the way, award yourself as milestones are reached. Awards are like affirmations from a dear loved one. They supply the on-going energy to stay the course and win. Journey awards are like memorial stones. They mark the memory. You did it!

KEY NOTES

LESSONS FROM THE KEYS Of LIFE:

RESILIENCE & EMPOWERMENT TO MOVE FORWARD

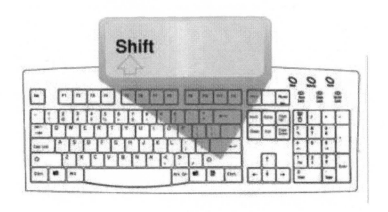

Shift Key:

Seasons change. Recognizing the seasons of life and relationships are important to your success. The **shift** is necessary in our jobs, careers, and small businesses in order to keep us cutting-edge. Updating our offices, marketing materials, or business goals may make the difference. The way we once did things, may no longer be relevant. This is true for relationships as well. Be willing to shift. The shift prevents stagnation. Keep moving forward.

KEY NOTES

LESSONS FROM THE KEYS Of LIFE:

RESILIENCE & EMPOWERMENT TO MOVE FORWARD

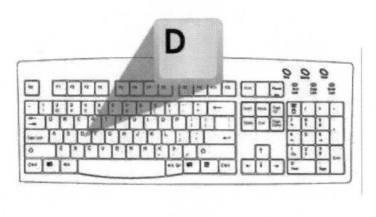

D Key:

Diligently work on you – your goals; your relationships; your purpose; and your progress. Get focused. See yourself winning – eyes open or eyes shut! Diligently run your race. Stay in your lane. Implement tools such as a planner, check list, and "To Do List" to help keep you focused. You will lose momentum and time concerning yourself with others' races. Your prize will only be found in your lane. The checkered flag is just ahead. Diligently pursue it. It's yours and it's in your lane. Run!

KEY NOTES

LESSONS FROM THE KEYS Of LIFE:

RESILIENCE & EMPOWERMENT TO MOVE FORWARD

Insert Key:

Building your knowledge base and skills are instrumental in keeping you cutting edge, relevant, and competitive. Be a life-long learner. Understand the trends and stay current in world events. Remain up to date in your industry. Participate in training classes and seminars. Listen to podcasts. Take an online course. Build your network by participating in networking events. Be sure to follow up with new contacts. Leverage relationships. Technology continues to evolve. Keep up! Stay current! "There's an app for that," is a current belief. There's also a You-Tube video for that. Help and resources are available. Take advantage of opportunities to improve you.

KEY NOTES

LESSONS FROM THE KEYS Of LIFE:

RESILIENCE & EMPOWERMENT TO MOVE FORWARD

Page Down Key:

Life sometimes presents us with seasons to move on. Personal and professional relationships may shift. Fulfillment on a job or within a career may dwindle. There's an inner knowing that things have changed. Stop to examine the signs. Is there something you need to do to breathe life back into the relationship? Is he or she still adding value to you? Is it time to move on to the fresh and the new? This applies to relationships and jobs/careers. Only you can provide the answer. **Page Down** is about moving forward. Take appropriate action. Move forward.

KEY NOTES

_____

_____

_____

_____

_____

_____

_____

_____

_____

_____

_____

_____

_____

LESSONS FROM THE KEYS Of LIFE:

RESILIENCE & EMPOWERMENT TO MOVE FORWARD

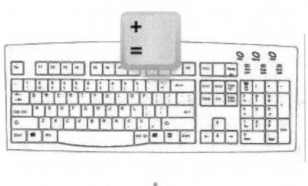

Plus (+) Key:

Self-improvement and self-care are great ways of promoting mental wellness. The benefits are enormous. In a day and age where work/life balance is an on-going struggle, taking care of yourself is imperative. Benefits include better health, better cognitive skills, more effective communication, confidence, assertiveness, less stress, etc. Investing in yourself through the vehicles of self-improvement and self-care are excellent ways of promoting "you." Self-improvement and self-care are unique to the individual. Find what works for you and implement it today.

KEY NOTES

_____

_____

_____

_____

_____

_____

_____

_____

_____

_____

_____

_____

_____

LESSONS FROM THE KEYS Of LIFE:

RESILIENCE & EMPOWERMENT TO MOVE FORWARD

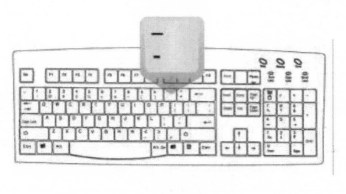

Minus (-) Key:

Enough! This is your reminder to be assertive. It is perfectly ok to say "no" when what you are being asked to do is not doable. OK, maybe "no" is not an option; at least negotiate a solution which will work for both parties. Sometimes, it is time to delegate. Identify tasks you are the best fit to fulfill and hire or assign someone to manage other tasks. It is unreasonable to manage it all. Attempting to manage it all is a sure-fire way to suffer burnout and stress, which could lead to several side effects such as poor health, insomnia, and depression. Know when to remove things from your "plate." Be willing to make the necessary changes. You will be glad you did.

KEY NOTES

_____

_____

_____

_____

_____

_____

_____

_____

_____

_____

_____

_____

_____

LESSONS FROM THE KEYS Of LIFE:

RESILIENCE & EMPOWERMENT TO MOVE FORWARD

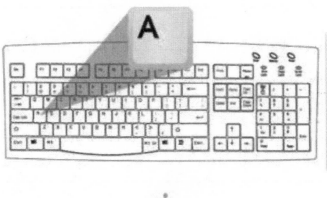

A Key:

Reserve time at the end of the day to evaluate your day. How would you rate your performance for the day in the home, on the job, in your relationships, and personally? Were you able to take care of all (or most) items on your "To Do" list? Did you earn an "A?" If not, don't be too hard on yourself. Award yourself and be proud of your accomplishments (big and small) and be determined to do better tomorrow. End the day in gratitude. Recall things which worked well and things which caused you to smile. Sleep well on a positive note.

KEY NOTES

_____

_____

_____

_____

_____

_____

_____

_____

_____

_____

_____

_____

_____

LESSONS FROM THE KEYS Of LIFE:

RESILIENCE & EMPOWERMENT TO MOVE FORWARD

O Key:

Get organized. Organization is an on-going process. Stay on top of things so things will not be found on top of you - weighing you down and stressing you out. Develop a system which works for you. A fellow-business owner, Judy Goode (founder of Goode's Cleaning Services) shared a cleaning system with me several years ago. She shared how her cleaning team tackles one area at a time when cleaning a room or facility. For example, they may start on the left side and remain in that area until the work is done. This spoke volumes to me and was instrumental in helping me develop a system of cleaning my desk and email inbox. Find what works for you and work it. Organization will help you maximize your time and increase productivity. Did I mention, it can also reduce or eliminate stress?

KEY NOTES

LESSONS FROM THE KEYS Of LIFE:

RESILIENCE & EMPOWERMENT TO MOVE FORWARD

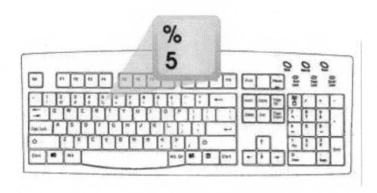

Percentage (%) Key:

Leadership is characterized by accountability. How committed are you to what matters most in your life? Take an honest assessment. Do you take responsibility for your actions? While personal accountability is very important, it is also important to have accountability partners in your life. This may be in the role of a mentor or business sponsor. While there are some things we can do and will do without the assistance of others; there are also those things which require assistance in order to increase the chances of success. It's time for results. Let's get our performance percentages up. It's time for increase.

KEY NOTES

LESSONS FROM THE KEYS Of LIFE:

RESILIENCE & EMPOWERMENT TO MOVE FORWARD

PRTSC – Print Screen Key

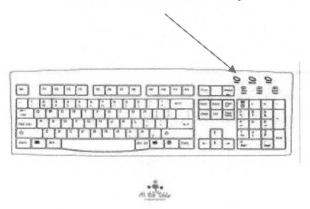

Print Screen Key:

Who are you? To answer this question, take a selfie. Study the image looking back at you. How would you describe yourself? Do you love yourself? Know that you are special. Your life is significant. Fulfilling your purpose in life is vital. Communicating who you are; what you want; and what you can do for others, with confidence, will open countless doors of opportunity. Be willing and ready to "sell yourself." The **print screen key** is your affirmation key. Speak well. Expect well. Settle for nothing less than the best. Enjoy the benefits.

KEY NOTES

_____

_____

_____

_____

_____

_____

_____

_____

_____

_____

_____

_____

LESSONS FROM THE KEYS Of LIFE:

RESILIENCE & EMPOWERMENT TO MOVE FORWARD

End Key

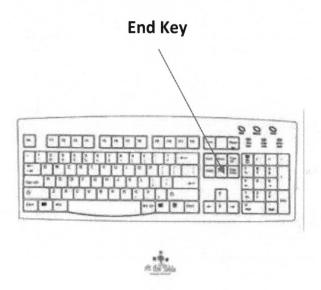

End Key:

End your day with proper rest. Strive for the recommended seven to eight hours of sleep. Awaking rejuvenated is a strong indication of meeting your body's sleep requirement. As you sleep, your body heals itself and cognitively, your memory can be strengthened. Awake with a great attitude and outlook on life. A good night's sleep is all it takes, sometimes, to figure things out or come up with your next creative idea. As a bonus, if possible, occasionally take a nap midday for a power boost. Limit the nap so that it will not prevent you from a good night's rest.

KEY NOTES

LESSONS FROM THE KEYS Of LIFE:

RESILIENCE & EMPOWERMENT TO MOVE FORWARD

Keep the Key Lessons Going

Now that I have shared my 24 keys, let's keep it going. There is so much more to be explored. In the following exercise, select a key, not previously shared, and allow your streams of consciousness to flow. Capture your thoughts in the field area located next to your selected key.

KEY	THOUGHTS

YOUR RESULTS DESIRED ARE POSSIBLE, BUT THEY DO REQUIRE YOUR "SKIN IN THE GAME."

~ Coach J Dianne Tribble

LESSONS FROM THE KEYS Of LIFE:

RESILIENCE & EMPOWERMENT TO MOVE FORWARD

WORK/ LIFE BALANCE BLEND

For many of us, we are living very busy lives. Attempting to manage everything that is required of us can be quite a juggling act. We hear so much today about work/life balance. In fact, it is one of those "currently trending" phrases. However, a more accurate term (in my opinion) would be work/ life blend or work/ life harmony.

So, what does this blend, or harmony look like? The blend or harmony consists of our faith and community impact; our sources of income; managing our finances; managing our health; and managing our relationships (family, friends, and professional).

What's missing in this picture? Self-care is the imperative missing component. Talking care of ourselves is essential to taking care of all the demands of work and life. Balance, blend, harmony, or whatever you chose to call it, begins with the individual. Neglecting ourselves places us in danger of jeopardizing our health; our jobs; our relationships; and our finances.

Self-care is all about taking care of yourself in a manner which produces joy, peace, soundness of mind, and rejuvenation. Self-care is unique to the individual. What works for one in restoring peace of mind, may not work for another. For example, something as simple as washing dishes or doing the laundry may work wonders for one person. For another, either of these tasks would be dreaded work. Find what works for you and implement it as soon as possible.

It's time to remove the stigma that self-care is selfishness. Self-care is vital to your success. The following image demonstrates the importance of self-care:

ME

WORK   **LIFE**

In the diagram, "ME" is represented by the tall standing frame. WORK is on one side and LIFE is on the other. In order to balance, blend, or harmonize, "ME" must maintain an erect posture. As you can see in the diagram, it all hinges on self-care. We must take care of ourselves spiritually, emotionally, mentally, physically, socially, etc.

At the Table

Life Coaching & Motivational Speaking Services
Unveiling Your Full Potential

PROCRASTINATION is the fruit of failure to plan or poor planning.

~ Coach J Dianne Tribble

www.atthetableinc.com

LESSONS FROM THE KEYS Of LIFE:

SELF-CARE TIPS

1. Pray and meditate.
2. Go on a date.
3. Sit down and do nothing. Exhale.
4. Take breaks throughout the day.
5. Listen to music and dance.
6. Journal your thoughts.
7. Work on a hobby.
8. Read something you desire to read.
9. Play games or work puzzles.
10. Spend quality time with friends.
11. Get a massage, along with a manicure and pedicure.
12. Watch a movie.
13. Go to a festival.
14. Do some retail therapy.
15. Affirm yourself.
16. Laugh.

LESSONS FROM THE KEYS Of LIFE:

RESILIENCE & EMPOWERMENT TO MOVE FORWARD

LIFE BLEND OR HARMONY TIPS

1. Communicate with your family members.
2. Share meals at the table. Practice healthy eating.
3. Share chores. Delegate.
4. Prioritize your time.
5. Keep a family calendar to track daily activities.
6. Schedule date nights.
7. Reserve time for intimacy with your spouse.
8. Take a break. Sit down and do nothing.
9. Manage your finances tracking statement due dates, banking reconciliations, and savings.
10. Avoid fees by paying bills prior to due date and using ATM machines which do not access fees.
11. Schedule maintenance appointments – health, dental, and vehicle in advance. Maintenance is cheaper than repair.
12. Schedule weekend getaways, mini-vacations, staycations, and vacations.
13. Wind down before bedtime.
14. Go to bed at the same time each night.
15. Keep electronic devices out of the bedroom (cell phones, iPads, and TV). The bedroom is for sleep and intimacy.
16. Journal before bedtime. Reflect on what went well during the day.
17. Affirm yourself and affirm each other.

LESSONS FROM THE KEYS Of LIFE:

RESILIENCE & EMPOWERMENT TO MOVE FORWARD

WORKPLACE TIPS

1. Arrive early. Allow adequate travel time to prevent running late.
2. Communicate with your family when work conflicts with home life.
3. Delegate whenever possible.
4. Make "To Do" lists.
5. Prioritize your time.
6. Take breaks.
7. Prepare for assignments, presentations, and tasks in advance to minimize stress.
8. Turn the music and talk radio off while commuting to work.
9. Represent your department and the organization well.
10. Demonstrate professionalism in your communications, work performance, and attire.

Small Business Owner Tips

1. Always be ready to pitch your business. Who are you? What do you do? Why should I do business with you?
2. Take advantage of networking opportunities.
3. Market your business.
4. Maintain a website and social media presence.
5. Join a professional business group for support.
6. Get a mentor or hire a Business Coach.

7. Take control of your time or your time will control you.
8. Track your mileage.
9. Track your assets and liabilities.
10. Keep business financials separate from personal or home finances.
11. Hire a CPA and a lawyer.
12. Purchase liability insurance.
13. Leverage relationships.
14. Participate in continuing education courses, webinars, and conferences in order to stay current in your industry.
15. Schedule work hours.

At the Table
Life Coaching & Motivational Speaking Services
Unveiling Your Full Potential

About the Author

Coach J Dianne Tribble, Award winning Health & Wellness and Business Coach, Motivational Speaker, Corporate Trainer, Business Consultant, and Published Author

2019 award recipient of the Public Service Award by ACHI Magazine and 1st Place award recipient of Best Business Coach/ Consultant by BEST (Black Entrepreneur SisTer) Society. 2019 Woman of Influence nominee by the Jacksonville Business Journal. Awarded the 2018 Health & Wellness Award for her impact in the community by ACHI Magazine Awards, Coach J Dianne Tribble is the CEO and founder of At the Table Life Coaching & Motivational Speaking Services LLC. In 2018, she also received a Certificate of Recognition for Women Who Lead by VITAS Healthcare and was voted #1 Life Coach in Jacksonville, FL by Expertise.com. In 2011 & 2015, she was the recipient of the Spirit of Service Award for her impact within the community by the University of Phoenix. She is a Certified

Professional Business & Health & Wellness Coach, Corporate Trainer, inspiring Motivational Speaker, published author, and a business start-up consultant. Her business ministry provides service solutions for:

- one-on-one and group Life Coaching, Family Dynamics Interventions, Business Coaching, and personal development services
- a thriving faith-based life coach certification program (approximately 110 men and women (internationally)
- Public speaking (internationally)
- Training and workshop development
- Business & professional consultations

Service to her community includes IMPACT Church, Executive President for the University of Phoenix Alumni North FL, PACE Center for Girls, Junior Achievement Girls North Florida, L.E.A.P. Women's Empowerment Group, PUSH Ministries, and Bosom Buddies (breast cancer awareness and support group). She is the co-founder of We Are Women In Business, a women's professional group. She is the founder of Coaches At the Table, a community of Life Coaches, where continuing education, networking, fellowship, and support are provided. She teaches continuing education classes for Duval County School System. As a Corporate Trainer, she provides health & wellness training for numerous companies in North East Florida, including TIAA Bank (formerly known as EverBank), JP Morgan Chase Bank, Merrill Lynch, Bank of America, Beaver Street Fisheries, Edward Waters College, C&S Wholesalers, Prudential Financial Services, etc. In addition, she provides training internationally via the web.

Coach J Dianne Tribble provides inspiring motivational public speaking services in faith-based organizations, in corporations, in specialty groups, and educational institutions.

Articles written by Coach J Dianne Tribble have been featured in Entrepreneurs Anchor Magazine, Program Success Magazine, and Ezine Articles. She has been featured numerous times on local TV broadcasts and radio stations in Jacksonville, FL and Atlanta, GA.

She resides in Jacksonville, FL with her husband, Larry, of 37 years. They are the proud parents of three successful adult children and one son-in-law.

At the Table
Life Coaching & Motivational Speaking Services
Unveiling Your Full Potential

Published Books by Coach J Dianne Tribble

- ❖ Lessons from the Keys
- ❖ The Curtain Opens
- ❖ The Essential "C" Experience
- ❖ Taking the Plunge
- ❖ Funnel Vision
- ❖ The Star Inside of You
- ❖ The Write Stuff: Journaling the Journey
- ❖ Managing My Time as I Manage Me
- ❖ Weave the Dream At the Table

Life Coaching & Motivational Speaking Services
Unveiling Your Full Potential

Contact Information

Book Coach J Dianne Tribble for your speaking engagements, workshops, training, and coaching needs. Our certification training programs include life coach certification and train-the-trainer certifications.

Business Name: At the Table Life Coaching & Motivational Speaking Services LLC

Website: **www.atthetableinc.com**

Business Line: (904) 613-8437

Email address: **coaching@atthetableinc.com**

Social Sites:

- LinkedIn: LinkedIn.com/in/jdiannetribble
- Face Book: Facebook.com/AtthetableLifeCoaching/
- Instagram: @atthetablewdi
- Twitter: @Atthetable_wDi
- Periscope: Atthetable_wDi

LESSONS FROM THE KEYS Of LIFE:

RESILIENCE & EMPOWERMENT TO MOVE FORWARD

Made in the USA
Columbia, SC
27 January 2022

54485558R00052